JUN 1 5 2016

THE NO SALT
COOKBOOK

THE NO SALT COOKBOOK

Emily George

NEW
HOLLAND

Dedicated to the three little people in my life;
Max, Lucy and Alice.

Contents

INTRODUCTION

Life was thrown into disarray for a while in 2011 while I was pregnant with my third child – I was diagnosed with Meniere's disease – a condition of the inner ear, disturbing balance and hearing. By the time I was diagnosed I was suffering daily vertigo attacks, had lost most of the hearing in one ear, and had constant tinnitus. Although currently incurable, Meniere's can be managed. For a lot of people, including me, a low sodium diet helps. And so began my new food journey...

Before being diagnosed with Meniere's disease, I didn't realize how much salt I actually consumed, not just in the extra I would add while cooking, but what was already in store bought ingredients such as sauces, condiments, cereals, bread, stocks, cheeses – the list goes on! It was a real wake up call for me as to what kind of food I was feeding not only myself, but my family. I quickly became used to food without salt, and even more so, ingredients that were low sodium. Everything started to taste so much better. Fresh herbs and spices became my new best friends and I loved knowing exactly what was going into my meals. Who would have thought salt free didn't have to be bland and boring after all!

Having always loved cooking I was forever on the lookout for new meals to create, and I started to realize that there was a distinct lack of good, flavorsome, salt free recipes available – or the ones that were salt free, still used high sodium ingredients. So I began to create my own, and this book emerged.

During the process, I have really enjoyed creating new dishes and discovering new flavors. Using ingredients that I previously didn't even know existed, or just didn't know what to do with. As a busy mum, I have tried to include a combination of some easy to prepare mid week meals, as well as dishes I proudly serve when entertaining. Now when I host friends for dinner and I tell them there is no salt in the meal, they just can't believe it.

This book is for anyone who needs to reduce their sodium intake due to medical reasons, or those just wanting to eat healthy food. If you are beginning your no salt journey, please give yourself a couple of weeks for your taste buds to regenerate and you will notice a huge difference in the flavors you can taste without the salt. I would also encourage you to try new herbs and spices that you might not have used before, and recipes with ingredients you might not be familiar with.

There is a great big world of delicious salt free food out there, so go and enjoy some today!

LITTLE BITES

Almond Energy Balls

These are so delicious and my current go-to snack! Most commercially bought snacks are very high in sodium so it is great to have these sitting in the fridge on hand. They keep well in an airtight container in the fridge for a few days. They have no gluten, no egg, no sugar and most importantly they are low in sodium. Coconut oil can turn solid in cooler weather, if this happens you can pop it in the microwave for a few seconds to melt it.

200 g (7 oz) almonds
40 g (1.5 oz) desiccated coconut
1 tbsp cocoa powder
1 tsp black chia seeds
1 tsp cinnamon
1 tsp nutmeg
½ an avocado, ripe
2 tbsp honey
1 tsp coconut oil

Makes about 30 balls

1. In a food processor, place the almonds and process until they are nearly ground, but still with a little texture.
2. Add the coconut, cocoa powder, chia seeds, cinnamon and nutmeg. Process for just a few seconds until combined.
3. Add the avocado, honey and coconut oil, and process until the mixture begins to bind.
4. Take the mixture and roll into small balls, then refrigerate for at least 30 minutes.

Rosemary Focaccia

A delicious simple Focaccia bread that is lovely as is, or to dip with my Hummus (page 22).

300 g (10.5 oz) all-purpose (plain) flour

1 tsp dry yeast

60 ml (2 fl oz) plus 2 tsp olive oil

200 ml (7 fl oz) warm water

2 cloves garlic, peeled and crushed

Few sprigs of rosemary

Olive oil to grease bowl

Makes 1 large focaccia

1. In a large bowl, add the flour. Make a well in the centre and add the yeast, 60 ml (2 fl oz) olive oil, and the 200 ml (7 fl oz) warm water.
2. Mix with a flat pallet knife to combine.
3. Roll the mixture out onto a lightly floured surface, and knead for 10 minutes until smooth, adding a little more flour if it starts to stick. Place the dough into a bowl that has been lightly oiled.
4. Cover with a clean tea towel and leave in a warm place for 1.5–2 hours, until the dough has doubled in size.
5. Punch the dough to knock it down in the bowl, and then take it out and place onto a flat 23 x 33 cm (13 x 9 in) baking tray lined with greaseproof paper. Roll out then use your hands to fit into the tray. Allow to rest again, for about 45 minutes until the dough rises again.
6. While the dough is resting, preheat the oven to 200°C (390°F).
7. Once the dough has risen, use your finger to poke little indents into the dough, then place sprigs of rosemary into the indents.
8. Mix the remaining 2 teaspoons of olive oil with the crushed garlic, and drizzle over the dough. Then sprinkle with a little water.
9. Bake for about 20 minutes. Serve warm.

Five Spice Chicken Nibbles

I also make this recipe using chicken wings, but drummers are better for kids and nibbles. The oven time would need to be increased for larger wing pieces.

If you can't find low sodium breadcrumbs, you can make your own by processing some low sodium homemade bread (see recipe on page 198).

1 kg (2.2 lb) chicken drumettes (or wings)
2 tsp Chinese five spice
115 g (4 oz) breadcrumbs, low sodium
2 tsp ground cumin
1 tsp ground cilantro (coriander) seeds
Freshly ground black pepper
70 g (2.5 oz) all-purpose (plain) flour
2 eggs, lightly beaten
Vegetable or olive oil, for frying

Serves 4

1. Preheat the oven to 180°C (350°F).
2. Make the crumb mixture by combining the Chinese five spice, breadcrumbs, cumin, cilantro and pepper. Mix well.
3. Coat the chicken drumettes lightly in flour, then dip the chicken in the beaten egg, then coat with the breadcrumb mixture.
4. Heat about 1 cm (½ in) of oil in a frying pan to a medium heat.
5. Add the chicken pieces to the pan and cook for 1–2 minutes on each side until they are nice and golden. Drain on absorbent paper.
6. Place the chicken drumettes on a tray and bake for about 10 minutes, or until cooked through.

Arancini Balls

Mozzarella is one of the few cheeses that generally has a low sodium content and is available in supermarkets.

¼ brown onion, chopped finely

2 garlic cloves, crushed

1 tbsp of olive oil

115 g (4 oz) arborio rice

500 ml (16 fl oz) chicken stock

80 g (3 oz) mozzarella, chopped into small pieces about 1 cm (½ inch) cubed

115 g (4 oz) breadcrumbs, low sodium

Olive oil, for frying

Makes about 12 balls

1. In a saucepan, gently fry the onion and garlic in a tablespoon of olive oil for 2 minutes, and then add the rice, stirring to combine.
2. In another saucepan, add the stock and bring it to a very gentle simmer.
3. Add the stock to the rice, one ladle at a time, and stir continuously. Once the stock has been absorbed, add another ladle, repeat until all stock has been absorbed. This will take 20–25 minutes.
4. Remove the rice from the heat and add half the mozzarella, stirring to combine. Allow to cool a little.
5. Using the remaining mozzarella, take a small piece in your hand and roll the rice mixture around the mozzarella to form a ball. Then roll the ball in breadcrumbs. Continue until all the mozzarella has been rolled into balls and coated in breadcrumbs.
6. In a pan heat a little olive oil to medium heat. Gently fry the balls for a couple of minutes until lightly golden brown all over and heated through so that the mozzarella is warmed and melted inside.

Tzatziki

The tzatziki flavor will improve if you leave it covered in the fridge for a couple of hours before serving. This is a great side dish and goes perfectly with my Rosemary Focaccia (page 15).

1 long cucumber, about 325 g (11.5 oz)
1 garlic clove, crushed
1 tbsp finely chopped mint
2 tsp lemon juice
500 g (17.5 oz) plain thick greek yogurt

Makes 650 g (23 oz)

1. Peel the cucumber and slice in half lengthways. Scoop out the seeds and discard. Chop the remaining cucumber into very small pieces.
2. Place the cucumber into a clean tea towel (or paper towel) and squeeze gently to remove the excess water. Repeat with a new towel if the cucumber still seems quite wet.
3. In a bowl add the garlic, mint and lemon juice, mix well.
4. Add the cucumber and yogurt and stir to combine.

Hummus

Once made, you can store hummus in an airtight container in the fridge for a few days.
To make it last a little longer, prevent air getting to the hummus by pouring a thin layer of olive oil over the top once in its container.
Make sure that the can of chickpeas is a no added salt variety.

420 g (15 oz) can cooked
   chickpeas (garbanzo), drained
   and rinsed
125 ml (4 fl oz) water
75 g (3 oz) tahini paste
1 tbsp lemon juice
1 tsp olive oil
1 tsp cumin
½ tsp paprika powder
1 garlic clove, peeled

Makes 450 g (1 lb)

1. Place all ingredients into a food processor and blend until smooth.

Basil Pesto

Most store bought pesto is loaded with salt. It is so easy to make your own salt free and healthy version! Once made, you can store this in an airtight container in the fridge for a few days. To make it last a little longer, prevent air getting to the pesto by pouring a thin layer of olive oil over the top once in its container. Pesto is delicious served on top of a grilled fish fillet, or you could toss through some warm pasta to make a quick and tasty meal.

1 large bunch of basil leaves,
  approximately 50 g (2 oz)
1 garlic clove, peeled
35 g (1.2 oz) pine nuts
60 ml (2 fl oz) olive oil
1 tsp lemon juice

Makes 140 g (5 oz)

1. Place all ingredients into a food processor and process until fully combined. Take care not to over process or the nuts will become too ground up and lose their texture.

Flat Bread

These flat breads are particularly great for serving with a simple curry (page 133) or pair up with some Tzatziki (page 21) or Hummus (page 22). You can use different oil to fry the bread, however I like to use rice bran as it tolerates high temperatures without burning or smoking.

5 tbsp plus 3 tsp all-purpose (plain) flour
½ tsp superfine (caster) sugar
1 tsp dried yeast
125 ml (4 fl oz) warm water
5 tbsp besan flour (chickpea flour)
½ tsp cumin
½ tsp ground cilantro (coriander) seeds
3 tsp olive oil
Rice bran oil, for frying

Makes about 8

1. In a large bowl, add 3 teaspoons of the all-purpose flour, then add the sugar, yeast and warm water. Mix well.
2. Place in a warm sunny spot and leave for around 20–25 minutes until it has foamed.
3. Then add the remaining 5 tablespoons of all-purpose flour, besan flour, cumin, cilantro and oil. Mix and then roll out onto a very lightly floured table. Knead lightly to form a dough, then place back in the bowl. Leave in a warm sunny place again, until the dough has doubled in size, around 25 minutes.
4. When ready, break off pieces of dough a little smaller than a golf ball in size. Roll out into thin flat circular pieces, about 15 cm (6 in) in diameter.
5. Prepare a frying pan to hot with some rice bran oil. Cook the flat bread in the pan for a couple of minutes each side, until they are nice and golden.

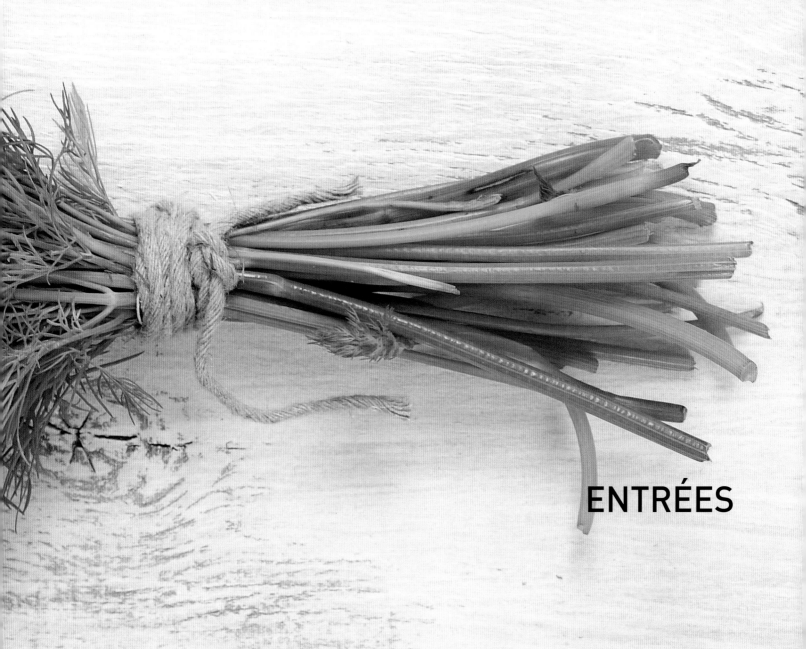

ENTRÉES

Chicken Skewers with Satay Sauce

A low sodium satay sauce is just about impossible to find! Thankfully the recent introduction of no added salt peanut butter in supermarkets made this recipe much easier to make.

Soak your wooden skewers in cold water for a few minutes before using them, this way they won't burn on the pan.

You could also serve these skewers with some Coconut Rice (page 163).

Chicken skewers

500 g (17.5 oz) chicken breast (or thigh) cut
   into 3 cm (1¼ in) cubes
1 tsp turmeric powder
Olive oil, for frying
Few drops sesame oil
1 tsp sesame seeds

Satay sauce

1 tbsp olive oil
1 red chili
1 garlic clove, crushed
1 tsp ground cilantro (coriander) seeds
1½ tsp cumin
Juice of 1 lime
1 square inch fresh ginger, grated
1 tsp brown sugar
3 tbsp peanut butter, no added salt variety
170 ml (5.7 fl oz) water

Coconut Rice to serve, if desired (page
   163)

Serves 4

Chicken skewers method

1. Thread the chicken pieces onto skewers.
2. Sprinkle the turmeric powder evenly over the chicken skewers.
3. Heat a little olive oil in a grill pan.
4. Fry the skewers in the grill pan for 3–4 minutes each side, or until cooked through, pouring a couple of drops of sesame oil over each skewer while cooking.
5. During the last couple of minutes of cooking scatter the sesame seeds over the skewers so that they toast just a little.

Satay sauce method

1. Heat olive oil to medium heat and add the chili and garlic. Fry for 1 minute.
2. Add the cilantro and cumin, fry 30 seconds.
3. Add the lime juice, ginger, brown sugar, peanut butter and water.
4. Simmer for 2–3 minutes and serve.

Deep Fried Chicken Wings

Ok, so this is definitely not the healthiest of meals being deep fried! But it is nice to have as an occasional treat. To make it a little healthier, you can shallow fry the chicken for a couple of minutes just to brown the outside, then finish off by baking in the oven at 200°C (390°F) for around 20 minutes.

300 g (10.5 oz) all-purpose (plain)
    flour
½ tsp white pepper
½ tsp turmeric powder
1 tsp garlic powder
1 tsp smoked paprika powder
250 ml (8 fl oz) buttermilk
1.5 kg (3.3 lb) chicken wings
Rice bran oil for deep frying (or
    vegetable oil)

Serves 6

1. In a large bowl mix the flour, white pepper, turmeric, garlic powder and paprika.
2. Pour the buttermilk into a clean bowl, and then dip a chicken wing into the milk until coated. Then transfer to the flour bowl and coat the chicken in the flour mixture. Repeat until all the chicken is coated in milk and flour.
3. Heat the oil in a deep fryer or saucepan to medium high heat and deep fry the chicken wings in small batches, for about 4 minutes each or until cooked through.

Simple Garlic and Chili Angel Hair

If you prefer less heat – just reduce the amount of chili or remove the seeds.
Add more or less of the cooking water at the end, depending on how dry the pasta is.

400 g (14 oz) dry angel hair pasta
4 tbsp olive oil
4 garlic cloves, crushed
2 large red chilis, chopped
Zest of a lemon

Serves 4

1. Cook the pasta in boiling water for 2 minutes. Once cooked, reserve 3 tablespoons of the cooking water, then drain the pasta.
2. Meanwhile, in a pan at medium heat, add the olive oil, garlic, chili and lemon zest and fry for 1 minute.
3. Add the pasta to the pan, and toss to combine. Add a few tablespoons of the cooking water and toss. Serve immediately.

Quinoa Crusted Shrimp with Chili and Lime Yogurt

Quinoa flakes make a great alternative to breadcrumbs, and have almost no sodium. Quinoa is also gluten free. I like to buy the shrimp (prawns) already peeled and de-veined, this saves a lot of time! If you don't like any sweetness in the yogurt, just leave out the honey completely. Shrimp do have a higher sodium content than other proteins, so I like to have them just now and again as a treat.

Yogurt

150 g (5 oz) Greek yogurt

Rind of 1 lime

1 small red chili, chopped finely
    with seeds in

1 tsp honey

Shrimps

400 g (14 oz) raw, peeled and
    de-veined shrimp (prawns)

2 eggs, lightly beaten

100 g (4 oz) quinoa flakes

Vegetable oil, for frying

Serves 4

Yogurt method

1. In a small bowl mix all the yogurt sauce ingredients together until combined. Refrigerate until you are ready to serve.

Shrimp method

1. Prepare the lightly beaten egg in one bowl, the quinoa flakes in another.
2. Dip the shrimp one at a time in the egg, then roll in the quinoa flakes. Repeat until all shrimp are coated.
3. Heat a little oil in a small pan on medium/high.
4. I suggest testing the oil heat and cooking time with just one shrimp first.
5. Fry the shrimp a few at a time so that the pan isn't over crowded.
6. They should only take a minute or so, on each side.
7. Serve the shrimp while still hot, with the yogurt dipping sauce.

Salmon and Dill Patties

Make sure you don't over boil the potatoes or they will become too soft to hold their shape when frying. These patties are quick and easy, great for lunches the next day and even the kids will eat them!

1 kg (2.2 oz) potato, peeled and cut into 4 cm (1½ in) pieces
½ brown onion, chopped finely
420 g (15 oz) can no added salt salmon, drained
2 tbsp flat leaf parsley, chopped
2 tbsp dill, chopped
Freshly cracked black pepper
125 g (4.5 oz) all-purpose (plain) flour
Vegetable or olive oil, for frying

Serves 4–6

1. Place the potatoes in a saucepan of cold water and bring to the boil, reduce heat to a gentle boil for a further 10 minutes.
2. Drain potatoes and mash, set aside to cool.
3. In a pan with a little oil, gently fry the onions for a couple of minutes until they begin to soften. Transfer onions to a large bowl, then add the salmon, parsley, dill, cracked pepper. Add the mashed potato and mix until well combined.
4. Take the potato mixture and form into pattie shapes approximately 1.5 cm (½ in) thick. Refrigerate for about 30 minutes – this helps them to hold their shape when frying.
5. Heat a little oil in a frying pan on medium heat. Sprinkle the flour onto a plate, and coat patties in a little flour on each side. Fry them in the pan for approximately 3 minutes on each side.

Lamb Parcels with Mint and Lemon

The best way to approach this recipe is to make the dough first, while that is rising, make the filling mixture. These parcels are so delicious, squeeze some lemon over them before eating!

Dough

300 ml (10 fl oz) water
2 tsp dried yeast
390 g (13.5 oz) all-
   purpose (plain) flour
1 tbsp olive oil
Extra olive oil for frying
Lemon wedges

Filling

1 small onion, finely
   chopped
1 clove garlic, chopped
500 g (17.5 oz) lamb
   mince
1 tbsp lemon juice
1 tsp sumac
1 tsp cumin
Freshly ground black
   pepper
3 tbsp curly leaf
   parsley, finely
   chopped
3 tbsp mint leaves,
   finely chopped
Olive oil, for frying

Serves 4–6

Dough method

1. Combine the water and yeast in a jug, stir to combine. Cover, set aside in a warm place for 5–10 minutes, or until bubbles begin to appear on the surface.
2. Sift the flour into a large bowl. Make a well in the centre and pour in the yeast mixture and olive oil. Mix to form a dough, then roll out onto a lightly floured surface.
3. Knead dough for 10 minutes, or until elastic. If the dough is a little dry, add a splash more water. Alternatively if it feels too wet, sprinkle a little extra flour.
4. Shape into 4 balls, and place onto an oiled baking tray. Cover with a clean tea towel and leave in a warm, sunny place for 30 minutes, or until the dough has doubled in size.
5. Take one piece of the dough and roll out into a thin rectangle shape (size dependant on the size of your frying pan).
6. Top one side with a few tablespoons of the mince mixture, folding the other side over the top. Pinch the edges to seal. Heat a large pan to medium heat. Brush each side of the parcel with olive oil before putting into the pan.
7. Cook for 3–4 minutes on each side, or until golden and crisp. Serve warm with lemon wedges.

Filling method

1. In a large pan on medium high heat with a little oil, add the onion and garlic, gently fry for 1 minute. Add the mince, and cook to brown.
2. Add the lemon juice, sumac, cumin and black pepper. Continue to simmer for 5 minutes or until the mince is cooked through.
3. Remove from the heat, allow to cool a little then stir through the parsley and mint. Set aside.

Mozzarella Mushrooms

A great vegetarian entrée, with minimal preparation time. To keep the overall sodium content low, make sure that your mozzarella is a low sodium variety.

4 large flat mushrooms

5 tbsp parsley, chopped

2 tbsp pine nuts, chopped roughly

2 garlic clove, crushed

4 tsp olive oil

40 g (1.5 oz) mozzarella, grated

½ tsp ground cilantro (coriander)

Makes 4

1. Preheat the oven to 200°C (400°F).
2. Prepare the mushrooms by trimming the stalk, making the area inside flat and easy to fill.
3. In a small bowl, combine the parsley, pine nuts, garlic, 2 teaspoons of olive oil, mozzarella and the ground cilantro. Mix well.
4. Spoon the mixture equally into the mushrooms.
5. Place them into a small baking tray and cover with foil.
6. Bake for 15 minutes.
7. Remove from the oven and take off the foil. Drizzle the remaining 2 teaspoons of olive oil over the top of the mushrooms, and return to the oven for a further 5 minutes, uncovered.
8. Remove and serve while still hot.

Lemongrass Chicken Skewers with Cilantro Dipping Sauce

The lemongrass won't be able to get through the chicken alone, so you need to make the holes first with a normal skewer. If you can't find long lemongrass, the shorter ones are still ok, you will just need more of them. Also look for the thinner stalks to make threading the chicken easier. You could also use skinless chicken thigh in place of chicken breast.

Dipping sauce

½ lemongrass stalk, finely chopped
Small red chili, finely chopped
1 tbsp chopped cilantro (coriander)
3 or 4 mint leaves, chopped finely
1 garlic clove, chopped finely
1 tbsp brown sugar
80 ml (2.7 fl oz) water
60 ml (2 fl oz) rice wine vinegar

Skewers

500 g (17.5 oz) skinless chicken breast
6 long lemongrass stalks, washed and outer layer removed
Oil, for frying
Rice, to serve, if desired

Serves 4–6

Dipping sauce method

1. To make the dipping sauce, add all the ingredients into a small bowl and stir until the sugar has dissolved. Set aside until needed.

Skewers method

1. Chop the chicken into 4 cm (1½ in) cubes.
2. Take the lemongrass and roll them firmly on the bench to release the flavor. Be careful not to bend them out of shape, just apply a firm pressure with your palms.
3. Prepare the lemongrass by using a sharp knife to trim the small end of the stalks at an angle. They should then look pointy and a bit like a spear.
4. Take your first piece of chicken. Using a bamboo or metal skewer, pierce straight through to make a small hole. Then take the lemongrass stalk and thread the chicken on.
5. Repeat this process for all the chicken. Cover skewers and refrigerate for at least an hour to allow flavor to develop.
6. Remove the chicken from the fridge 5 minutes before you are ready to cook. Prepare a grill pan to medium high heat with a little oil. Cook the skewers for about 4 minutes on each side, or until chicken is cooked through.
7. Serve skewers with the dipping sauce and white rice.

Pan Fried Gnocchi with Sage and Burnt Butter

You will need a potato ricer to make these gnocchi beautiful and light.

500 g (17.5 oz) potatoes with skins on

90 g (3.2 oz) all-purpose (plain) flour

About 15 sage leaves

50 g (2 oz) unsalted butter

Extra flour for dusting

Serves 4

1. In a saucepan of boiling water, add the potatoes still in their skins. Boil for 15–20 minutes, or until a knife easily goes into the potato. Drain the potatoes and peel off their skins. Push each potato through the ricer while they are still hot, then set aside to cool completely.

2. Once the potato is cool, turn it out onto a clean bench which has been lightly floured. Add the flour, and gently bring together to form the dough. Try to handle the dough as little as possible and stop as soon as it has formed.

3. Split the dough into 4 balls, and sprinkle a little flour onto your bench. Take the first ball and roll it out into a thin log shape. Using a knife, cut the gnocchi into individual pieces but cutting and flicking each one off the end of the log. Place the gnocchi on a tray while you make the rest. Repeat until all the gnocchi pieces have been made.

4. In a large medium hot frying pan, add the butter and sage leaves, add the gnocchi and fry for a couple of minutes until the outside is golden and the sage crispy.

5. Depending on the size of your pan, you will probably have to cook the gnocchi in 2 or 3 batches. (This will also mean splitting the sage leaves and butter into the same amount of batches).

Roasted Stuffed Onions

Roasting onions this way makes them beautifully sweet and soft.
Removing the inner layers can be a little fiddly, but using the point of a small sharp knife works well.

4 small brown onions
(300 g/10.5 oz)
2 tbsp pine nuts, roughly
chopped
6 or 7 tbsp parsley, chopped
about 25 g (1 oz)
1 garlic clove, chopped
25 g (1 oz) unsalted butter,
melted
½ tsp ground cilantro (coriander)
seeds
Freshly cracked black pepper

Makes 4

1. Preheat the oven to 200°C (350°F).
2. Wrap the onions in foil, place on a baking tray and bake for
40 minutes. Remove the foil and peel away the skins.
3. With a small sharp knife, cut just the very top of the onions off,
then carefully remove (and set aside) the inner layers of the
onions, leaving the outer 2 or 3 layers.
4. Take about half of the onion layers you have set aside, and chop
into small pieces.
5. In a bowl, mix together the chopped onion, pine nuts, parsley,
garlic, butter, ground cilantro seeds and pepper.
6. Carefully spoon the mixture into the onions. Return the onions
to the baking tray, and bake in the oven, uncovered, for a further
10 minutes.

Corn Fritters with Tarragon

A fresh Sunday breakfast idea, or a little brunch, these fritters are simple and delicious.
You could also deep fry these fritters if you would like to be a little naughty!
Make sure your corn is a no added salt variety.

410 g (14 oz) can corn kernels
2 eggs, at room temperature
1 tsp ground cumin
1 tsp yeast
3 tbsp all-purpose (plain) flour
Vegetable oil, for frying
150 ml (5 fl oz) sour cream
1 tbsp fresh tarragon, chopped
Avocado slices and diced tomato
    to serve.

Makes about 8

1. In a mixing bowl, lightly beat the eggs. Add the cumin, yeast and flour.
2. Drain the corn and rinse in a colander. Add to the mixing bowl and stir to combine.
3. Cover with plastic wrap and set aside in a warm place for about 20 minutes.
4. Heat a frying pan to medium heat and add a little oil.
5. Drop tablespoons full of mixture into the pan and press gently to flatten.
6. Fry for about a minute on each side, then place on a warm plate. Continue to cook the remaining mixture.
7. Place the sour cream into a little dish to serve, sprinkling the chopped tarragon on top.
8. Serve with some diced tomato and avocado slices, if desired.

SOUPS

Broccoli Soup

A wholesome dairy free soup that is light, yet still filling.

1 brown onion, chopped

2 garlic cloves, chopped

2 celery stalks, chopped

1 tsp ground cilantro (coriander) seeds

1 tsp cumin

1 litre (1¾ pints) low sodium chicken stock

400 g (14 oz) white potatoes, peeled and cubed

250 ml (8 fl oz) water

500 g (17.5 oz) broccoli florets

Makes 2 litres (3½ pints)

1. In a saucepan over medium heat, fry the onion, garlic and celery for 4 minutes, stirring occasionally.
2. Add the ground cilantro seeds and cumin; fry for another 2 minutes, stirring occasionally.
3. Add the stock, potatoes and water. Bring to the boil, and then reduce to a simmer. Simmer for 10 minutes with the lid on.
4. Add broccoli and return to the boil. Reduce again to a simmer, for 5 minutes with the lid on, or until vegetables are soft.
5. Remove from the heat and blend until smooth.

Cabbage and Borlotti Bean Soup

This is such a hearty winter warmer! For a faster version of this soup, you could use one can of borlotti beans that have been drained and rinsed, making sure that they are a no added salt variety. The simmer time can then be reduced to 30 minutes. The consistency of this soup is quite thick, although you can thin it out a little with water if you prefer.

1 tbsp olive oil
1 carrot, peeled and sliced
2 celery stalks, chopped
1 onion, chopped
1 tsp ground cilantro (coriander) seeds
750 ml (24 fl oz) water
500 ml (16 fl oz) low sodium chicken stock
350 g (12.5 oz) cabbage, chopped roughly
185 g (6.5 oz) dry borlotti beans
Freshly cracked black pepper

Makes 1.5 litres (2½ pints)

1. In a large saucepan over medium heat, add the oil, carrot, celery, onion and cilantro seeds, gently fry for 4–5 minutes, stirring frequently.
2. Add the water, stock, cabbage and beans. Bring to the boil, and then reduce to a gentle simmer.
3. Simmer for 2 hours with the lid on. Stir occasionally, and skim any scum that sits on the surface.
4. Remove from the heat, and blend until smooth.
5. Add some freshly cracked black pepper to serve.

Mushroom Soup

Dried Shiitake mushrooms are available from most supermarkets, in the Asian food section.
Shiitake mushrooms have a very distinct earthy, nutty flavor.
Make sure your white beans are the no added salt variety.

20 g (¾ oz) dried shiitake
   mushrooms
500 ml (17.5 fl oz) hot water
500 ml (17.5 fl oz) low sodium
   chicken stock
400 g (14 oz) can white beans
   (cannellini), rinsed and drained
2 sprigs thyme, leaves stripped
125 g (4.5 oz) sour cream

Makes 1 litre (1¾ pints)

1. Place the dried shiitake mushrooms in a bowl and cover with the hot water. Leave to soak for 10 minutes.
2. In a saucepan, add the mushrooms and their soaking water, chicken stock, white beans and thyme. Bring to the boil, and then gently simmer for 15 minutes.
3. Remove from the heat. Blend the soup until smooth.
4. Add the sour cream and serve.

Potato and Leek Soup

You could also use low sodium vegetable stock instead of chicken stock.

30 g (1 oz) unsalted butter

1 leek, sliced

1 garlic clove, crushed

500 g (17.5 oz) potato, peeled and cut into 5 cm (2 in) pieces

500 ml (17 fl oz) low sodium chicken stock

250 ml (8 fl oz) water

125 ml (4 fl oz) thin pouring cream

Makes 1.5 litres (2½ pints)

1. In a saucepan over low/medium heat, add the butter, leek and crushed garlic.
2. Cook gently for 5 minutes, stirring frequently. The leeks should begin to fall apart, do not allow the leeks to brown, just to soften.
3. Add the potato, chicken stock, water and bring to the boil.
4. Reduce to a rapid simmer for 15 minutes, or until the potato is soft.
5. Remove from the heat and using a stick blender, carefully blend until smooth.
6. Add the cream and stir to combine.

Pumpkin Soup

Use a knife to check that the vegetables are soft and cooked through. You could also use vegetable stock instead of chicken stock, if you prefer.

800 g (1.7 lb) butternut pumpkin, roughly chopped into 5 cm (2 in) cubes

250 g (9 oz) potato (about 2 medium size) roughly chopped into 5 cm (2 in) cubes

1 litre (1¾ pints) low sodium chicken stock

250 ml (8 fl oz) water

½ tsp ground nutmeg

80 ml (2.5 fl oz) thickened cream

Freshly ground black pepper

Makes 2 litres (3½ pints)

1. In a large saucepan add the pumpkin, potatoes, chicken stock and water. Cover and bring to the boil.
2. Reduce heat and simmer, uncovered, for 20 minutes.
3. Remove from the heat and carefully blend until smooth using a hand held stick blender.
4. Add the nutmeg, thickened cream and black pepper, stirring to combine.

Roasted Tomato Soup

This delicious tomato soup is made by using the Semi-Dried Tomatoes recipe on page 196.

1 small brown onion, chopped
2 garlic cloves, crushed
Olive oil, for frying
250 g (9 oz) semi-dried tomato, chopped (about 14 halves from recipe page 196)
500 ml (16 fl oz) low sodium vegetable stock
Freshly ground black pepper

Makes 700 ml (1¼ pints)

1. In a saucepan on medium heat, gently fry the onion and garlic in a little olive oil for 2 minutes.
2. Add the tomato halves and stock.
3. Bring to the boil, then reduce the heat and simmer for 15 minutes with the lid on.
4. Remove from the heat and allow to cool slightly. Blend until smooth. Add some cracked black pepper to taste.

Cucumber Gazpacho

I love this cold cucumber gazpacho in the middle of summer, it is so light and refreshing, and bursting with flavor.

3 medium cucumbers (400 g/ 14 oz), chopped roughly
20 g (¾ oz) mint leaves (large handful)
1 garlic clove
½ an avocado
2 tsp lemon juice
150 g (5 oz) plain Greek yogurt
Freshly cracked black pepper

Makes 600 ml (20 fl oz)

1. In a food processor, add all of the ingredients, process until smooth. Pour into a container and refrigerate for at least an hour. Serve cold.

SALADS

Cucumber Sesame Salad

This salad is best when the cucumbers are cold straight from the fridge.
A simple, elegant and refreshing summer salad!

2 tsp sesame seeds

3 medium size cucumbers, about
  450 g (1 lb)

3 tsp chopped cilantro
  (coriander)

½ tsp sesame oil

2 tsp olive oil

2 tsp white vinegar

Serves 4

1. In a pan, gently toast the sesame seeds for a couple of minutes over a medium heat, until they start to turn golden. Remove from the heat and set aside.

2. Chop the cucumbers into cubes. In a bowl, mix the chopped cucumber, cilantro, oils, vinegar and most of the toasted sesame seeds until well combined.

3. Sprinkle the remaining sesame seeds on top of the salad.

Four Bean Salad

This salad is a great one to prepare a few hours before it is needed – just remember to set the dressing aside until you are ready to serve. It looks amazing and is really simple to prepare.
Make sure the beans are a no added salt variety.

400 g (14 oz) can four bean mix
2 carrots, chopped finely
3 celery stalks, chopped finely
¼ red onion, chopped finely
3 tsp curly leaf parsley, finely
   chopped
Juice of 1 lemon
1 tbsp olive oil

Serves 4–6

1. Drain the can of beans into a colander and rinse well under cold water. Place in a large mixing bowl.
2. Add the carrot, celery, onion and parsley to the bowl, mix well.
3. Combine the lemon juice and olive oil, mix into the salad just before serving.

Arugula and Mango Salad

Arugula (rocket) is my hands down favorite salad leaf variety – its bitterness is perfectly balanced out by the sweet mango in this recipe.

Dressing
10 mint leaves, chopped
2 tbsp flat leaf parsley, chopped
2 tbsp olive oil
2 tsp balsamic vinegar

Salad
2 ripe mangos, peeled and cut
   into 1.5 cm (½ in) cubes
150 g (5 oz) arugula (rocket)
   leaves

Serves 4

1. For the dressing, mix the chopped mint and parsley into a small bowl with the oil and balsamic vinegar.
2. In a large bowl place the arugula leaves and mango.
3. Add the dressing to the arugula bowl, toss gently and serve.

Salmon Pasta Salad

Sour cream or crème fraiche work equally well for this cold pasta salad – just use whichever you prefer. Make sure that your salmon can is the no added salt variety.

100 g (3.5 oz) dried penne pasta

1 bunch asparagus (about 10) ends trimmed, then cut in 2.5 cm (1 in) pieces

100 g (3.5 oz) snow peas, cut in 2.5 cm (1 in) pieces

210 g (7.5 oz) can salmon, drained and flaked

2 tbsp sour cream

2 tbsp chopped dill

1 tbsp lemon juice

Serves 4

1. Cook the pasta in a large saucepan of boiling water, for the time stated on packet directions, adding the asparagus and snow peas for the final 2 minutes of cooking time. Drain and refresh under cold water, drain again and set aside in a large bowl to cool.
2. Add the salmon to the pasta bowl.
3. Mix the sour cream, dill and lemon juice in a small bowl until smooth, and then add to the pasta.
4. Stir gently until combined, and all the pasta is coated.

Warm Beef Salad with Cilantro Dressing

Finally, a dish with asian flavors, but without all the sodium!
Make sure you prepare and chop all the herbs and vegetables beforehand, so that it is fast and easy to assemble once your beef is cooked.

Dressing

5 cm (2 in) long stalk of lemongrass, finely chopped

1 small red chili, chopped with seeds included

1 tbsp cilantro (coriander), chopped

1 small garlic glove, crushed

1 tbsp brown sugar

80 ml (3 fl oz) water

60 ml (2 fl oz) rice wine vinegar

Beef salad

250 g (9 oz) sirloin beef steak

¼ carrot, cut into matchsticks

¼ cucumber, cut into matchsticks

Mint leaves, about 4 or 5, chopped

100 g (3.5 oz) mixed spinach and arugula (rocket) leaves

½ red onion, chopped

50 g (2 oz) Vermicelli (Glass noodles)

Serves 4

Dressing method

1. Add all of the ingredients for the dressing into a bowl, and stir until all of the sugar has dissolved. Set aside.

Beef salad method

1. Heat a grill pan to high.
2. Add the sirloin and cook on each side for 2–3 minutes. Remove and rest.
3. Soak the noodles in a bowl of boiling water for 3–4 minutes, then drain and rinse under cold water.
4. In a bowl, place the carrot, cucumber, mint, spinach, arugula and onion. Add the noodles and mix well. Pour the dressing over the salad and toss.
5. Cut the steak into slices, place on top of noodle salad.

Orange and Fennel Salsa

Don't worry about slicing the orange too close to the rind, it won't be wasted as you will use all the left over juice in the dressing.

3 oranges

3 medium size fennel

1 tbsp parsley, finely chopped

2 tsp olive oil

Serves 4–6

1. Prepare the oranges by first cutting them in half, then quarters.
2. Slice the orange away from the rind (keep the rind), and dice the orange into small cubes. Add to a bowl.
3. Cut the fennel in half, and remove the hard core. Finely dice the fennel, then add to the oranges.
4. Add the chopped parsley and the oil.
5. Squeeze out all of the juice from the orange rind over the salad. Toss to combine and serve.

Herbed Lamb Meatball Salad

You can use any kind of lettuce leaves you like for this salad. If you cannot source any low sodium breadcrumbs, you can easily make your own, just throw some low sodium bread (page 198) into a food processor for fast crumbs.

Yogurt dressing

270 g (9.5 oz) Greek style yogurt
1 tbsp of finely chopped mint, plus a
   few extra leaves to garnish
1 tbsp lemon juice
1 tsp honey

Salad

Olive oil, for frying
¼ onion, finely chopped
2 garlic cloves, crushed
1 tbsp paprika powder
1 tbsp cumin
500 g (17.5 oz) lamb mince
1 egg, lightly beaten
40 g (1.5 oz) low sodium
   breadcrumbs
Cos lettuce leaves washed and dried
1 small cucumber, sliced
¼ red bell pepper (capsicum), sliced
1 small red onion, thinly sliced

Serves 4

Yogurt method

1. Combine the yogurt, mint, lemon juice and honey in a small bowl. Keep chilled until serving.

Salad method

1. Preheat the oven to 180°C (350°F)
2. Heat 1 tablespoon olive oil in a frying pan over medium heat. Add the onion and cook for 2 minutes, stirring, until soft.
3. Add the garlic, paprika and cumin, and cook for a further 1 minute. Remove from heat and transfer to a large bowl. Cool slightly.
4. Add the lamb mince, egg and breadcrumbs and mix thoroughly. Use your hands to shape meatballs, this mixture will make approximately 20 meatballs.
5. Place the frying pan back over medium heat, add more oil if necessary.
6. Cook the meatballs in batches, turning regularly, for approximately 2–3 minutes, until browned.
7. Place meatballs on a baking tray and bake in the oven for approximately 6 minutes.
8. Arrange the lettuce leaves, cucumber, bell pepper, red onion and meatballs on a serving plate. Top with the yogurt dressing, and extra mint leaves.

Balsamic Beetroot and Ricotta Salad

Beetroot becomes so sweet when roasted, and tastes beautiful with the mint leaves. You could also roast and peel the beetroot the day before you need them, just store them in an airtight container in the fridge.

4 medium beetroot (about
  800 g/1.8 lb), washed
2 cloves garlic
2 tsp balsamic vinegar
2 tbsp ricotta
Small handful of mint leaves

Serves 4–6

1. Preheat the oven to 180°C (350°F).
2. Leave the skin on the beetroots and place them into a deep roasting tray.
3. Take the garlic and with the back of a knife, squash them a little while still in their skin. Then place them in the roasting tray also.
4. Pour enough water into the tray so that it comes about a third of the way up the sides of the beetroot.
5. Cover with tin foil and bake for 1 hour.
6. Remove from the oven and let the beetroot cool.
7. Once the beetroot is cool, carefully peel the skins off (they should slide off easily). Make sure that you wear gloves to do this so that your hands don't get stained pink!
8. Once the skin has been removed, chop the beetroot into small pieces, and place into a serving bowl.
9. Spoon over the balsamic vinegar and toss to coat. Drop little blobs of the ricotta over the beetroot, then place the mint leaves on top.

Broccolini and Almond Salad

To maintain the crunch, it is really important to refresh the broccolini in iced water to stop the cooking process.

2 tbsp flaked almonds
2 bunches broccolini, ends
    trimmed
2 spring onions (scallions), sliced
1 tbsp olive oil
1 tbsp lemon juice
Freshly ground black pepper

Serves 4

1. In a heavy based pan over medium heat, toast the almond flakes for 2–3 minutes, or until they just begin to brown. Shake them regularly so they do not burn. Set aside.
2. Put the broccolini into a saucepan of boiling water for 3 minutes, then drain and refresh in a bowl of ice water. Drain again and place into a bowl.
3. Add the almonds, spring onions, oil, lemon juice and black pepper, and toss to combine.

Gourmet Tomato Salad

This tomato salad looks great when you can use a variety of different colored and shaped tomatoes. Perfect for summer and quick to prepare.

750 g (26.5 oz) mixed gourmet
tomatoes
100 g (3.5 oz) bocconcini balls,
sliced in half
4 tbsp basil pesto (recipe page
23)
Olive oil, to drizzle

Serves 4–6

1. Slice the larger tomatoes and cut the smaller ones in half.
2. Arrange them on a platter, then scatter the bocconcini halves over the tomatoes.
3. Take a teaspoon and drop dollops of the pesto on the salad.
4. Finish with a drizzle of olive oil over the platter.

MAINS

Baked Salmon Parcels

These salmon parcels not only look great but make for a really healthy meal. Serve them still wrapped up straight from the oven, and let your guests unfold their impressive looking parcels!

4 x 200 g (7 oz) salmon fillets
2 garlic cloves, peeled and sliced
1 lemon, thinly sliced
A few fresh dill sprigs
Freshly ground black pepper
2 tsp olive oil

Serves 4

1. Preheat the oven to 180°C (350°F).
2. Cut 4 pieces of baking paper to approximately 30 x 20 cm (12 x 8 in).
3. Lay one salmon fillet (skin down if you have skin) onto one piece of the baking paper. Place the garlic, lemon, dill and pepper on top of the salmon and then drizzle with a little olive oil. Repeat for the remaining fillets.
4. Bring up the 2 long sides of the paper and fold over a few times. Bring up the other 2 sides of paper and fold over to form a parcel.
5. Place the four parcels on a flat baking tray and bake in the oven for 10 minutes.

Chicken and Semi-Dried Tomato Pasta

This recipe is a great way to use any left over roast chicken from page 135, and the tomatoes from page 196. A quick meal using leftovers and minimal ingredients.

200 g (7oz) dry pasta shells

65 g (2.5 oz) cooked chicken, shredded

5 semi-dried tomato halves, (see page 196) chopped

85 ml (2.8 fl oz) thickened cream

Fresh basil leaves

Freshly cracked black pepper

Serves 4

1. Cook the pasta shells in boiling water for the time directed on packet, drain and return to the saucepan off the heat.
2. Add the shredded chicken, chopped tomatoes and cream. Stir to combine well.
3. Serve in bowls with fresh basil and cracked black pepper to garnish.

Fennel Pork Cutlets

Try serving with mashed potato and a green salad for a delicious meal. You can easily substitute the pork cutlets for pork chops if you prefer. To grind the fennel seeds use either a mortar and pestle or a spice/herb grinder, until seeds become a powder.

4 pork cutlets
2 tsp fennel seeds, ground
Freshly ground black pepper
2 tbsp olive oil
2 garlic cloves, crushed
1 fennel bulb, core removed,
   trimmed and sliced

Serves 4

1. Press the ground fennel seeds onto each side of the cutlets, and then season with the black pepper. Using half the olive oil, drizzle over each cutlet.
2. Heat the remaining oil in a pan to medium heat. Gently fry the garlic and fennel for 2 minutes. Reduce the heat to medium low and continue to fry for a further 5 minutes until the fennel softens. Set aside the fennel and garlic in a bowl.
3. In the same pan, cook the pork cutlets for about 4 minutes on each side (depending on thickness). Remove from the pan and let the pork rest for 2 minutes on a plate.
4. To serve, place the fennel and garlic on top of the cutlets.

Ginger and Cilantro Chicken Patties

Egg free and gluten free! These patties are great for anyone avoiding breadcrumbs or egg as they don't contain either, but still hold their shape quite well when cooking. You could also shape these into small meatball size if you prefer, even add them to a salad. You can leave the chili out if making these for kids.

2 tsp fresh ginger, finely chopped
2 garlic cloves, chopped
1 small red chili, finely chopped
2 tbsp finely chopped cilantro (coriander)
Juice of one lime
500 g (17.5 oz) chicken mince
Oil for frying

Serves 4

1. Place all ingredients except for the chicken in a large mixing bowl, and mix.
2. Add the chicken mince and combine until mixed well, then set aside to marinade for about 15 minutes. (For even better flavor, leave for a few hours in the fridge).
3. Heat a pan to medium heat and add a little oil.
4. Shape the mince to form patties about 1.5 cm (½ in) thick, then fry in the pan for about 2 minutes each side.

Mushroom Stroganoff

This is a great vegetarian meal that really fills you up. You can prepare this dish hours in advance – just leave out the sour cream. Keep the mixture in the fridge until ready to serve, reheat gently in a saucepan until hot, then add the sour cream. Button mushrooms can also be used in place of swiss brown.

100 g (3.5 oz) unsalted butter

2 garlic cloves, crushed

2 small brown onions, chopped

1 tbsp caraway seeds, ground

1 tbsp paprika powder

400 g (14 oz) swiss brown
  mushrooms, sliced

250 ml (8 fl oz) water

125 g (4.5 oz) sour cream

2 tbsp chopped parsley

Serves 4

1. In a saucepan on a medium heat, add the butter, garlic and chopped onion and cook for 2 minutes.
2. Add the ground caraway, paprika powder and mushrooms; cook for 1 minute.
3. Add the water and gently simmer for 5 minutes.
4. Remove from the heat, add the sour cream and stir until just combined. Garnish with chopped parsley.

Pine Nut Crusted Lamb Rack

I like to use a pan that can go straight from the stove top into the oven – saves time and washing up!
If you feel the paste is too dry, add a little more olive oil.
You can also use pistachio nuts instead of pine nuts for a different taste.

70 g (3 oz) pine nuts, chopped

1 garlic clove, crushed

2 tbsp curly leaf parsley, finely chopped

2 tbsp rosemary, finely chopped

1 tsp lemon zest

1 tbsp lemon juice

1 tbsp olive oil

Freshly cracked black pepper

Extra oil for frying

850 g (1.5 lb) lamb rack (preferably frenched so there is less fat)

Serves 4

1. Preheat the oven to 180°C (350°F).
2. In a bowl, add the nuts, garlic, parsley, rosemary, lemon zest, lemon juice, oil and black pepper. Mix to combine well and set aside.
3. Heat a grill pan to medium high heat and add a little oil. Once hot, place the lamb rack onto the pan to seal the meat. Sear for 2–3 minutes on each side until it has developed a nice golden color.
4. Remove from the heat. Take a spoonful of the oil mixture and press onto the lamb. Use all of the mixture, ensuring that it is evenly distributed across the top of the meat.
5. Bake in the oven for 30 minutes. Remove and cover loosely with foil, allow to rest for 10 minutes before serving.

Roast Pumpkin Pappardelle

A lovely light pasta dish with a variety of textures. You can use any variety of pumpkin you prefer.

500 g (17.5 oz) pumpkin, peeled
  and cut into 1.5 cm (½ in) cubes
1 tbsp vegetable oil
400 g (14 oz) pappardelle pasta
2 garlic clove, crushed
50 g (2 oz) unsalted butter
30 g (1 oz) pine nuts
Small handful of sage leaves

Serves 4

1. Preheat the oven to 200°C (390°F).
2. Place the pumpkin pieces in a roasting tray and drizzle with the vegetable oil. Bake for about 25 minutes, turning pieces once halfway through the cooking time.
3. Cook the pappardelle pasta in boiling water for the time directed on the packet, drain and return to saucepan (off the heat).
4. In a small pan, fry the garlic in the butter for 1 minute on medium heat.
5. Add the pine nuts and sage leaves; stir to ensure the sage is coated in butter, then simmer for a further 2 minutes.
6. Put the roasted pumpkin into the saucepan with the pasta, and then gently mix through the sage butter and pine nuts. Transfer to bowls or serving platter.

Sticky Spiced Pork Rashers

These sweet rashers are great served with rice and stir fried vegetables.

700 g (1.5 lb) pork rashers
125 ml (4 fl oz) malt vinegar
1 tbsp golden syrup
70 g (2.5 oz) brown sugar
1 garlic clove, chopped finely
½ tsp Chinese five spice

Serves 4

1. Place the pork rashers in a large bowl.
2. In a heavy based saucepan, add all the ingredients except for the pork, and heat over low heat until the sugar and syrup has dissolved, stirring frequently.
3. Pour the mixture over the pork rashers. Set aside to marinade for about 20 minutes (at room temperature).
4. Heat a grill pan (or barbecue) to medium high. Remove the pork from the marinade (reserve marinade in bowl). Cook the rashers for about 4 minutes on each side, then set aside.
5. Take the marinade and let it simmer for 6–8 minutes on the stovetop, or until it thickens to desired consistency. Pour over pork rashers and serve.

Veal Fillets with Polenta

This is one of the fastest meals to prepare, making it a great midweek option.
I like to serve the veal with polenta – there are quick cook varieties which are ready in less than five minutes, found in most supermarkets.

4 veal cutlets

2 tsp olive oil

2 tbsp dried tarragon

2 tsp garlic powder

Bunch of spinach leaves

Polenta, to serve if desired

Serves 4

1. Heat a grill pan to medium high heat.
2. Lay the veal fillets on a plate and drizzle with half the oil. Then sprinkle half the garlic powder and dried tarragon over. Turn the fillets over, and repeat on the other side with the remaining oil, garlic powder and dried tarragon.
3. Place the cutlets in the grill pan and cook for about 4 minutes on each side, remove to rest on a warm plate.
4. In the same pan, add the spinach leaves and cook for a minute or so to just wilt them.

Red Wine Casserole

Slow cooking is a great way to use cheaper cuts of meat like gravy beef. The flavors in this casserole will improve over time so this is definitely one you could make the day before, refrigerate overnight, and gently reheat just before serving.

40 g (1.5 oz) all-purpose (plain) flour

500 g (17.5 oz) gravy beef, diced into 2.5 cm (1 in) pieces

Oil for frying

2 cloves garlic, chopped

4 french onion shallots, peeled and left whole

2 carrots, peeled and cut into 2.5 cm (1 in) pieces

2 celery sticks, sliced in 5 mm (¼ in) thickness

40 g (1.5 oz) unsalted butter

500 ml (16 fl oz) low sodium beef stock

250 ml (8 fl oz) red wine

2 tbsp no added salt tomato paste

Cracked black pepper

A few large sprigs of thyme

Serves 4

1. Preheat the oven to 180°C (350°F). Have a large casserole dish with a lid ready.
2. Place the flour into a bowl, and add the beef. Toss the beef well until every piece is covered in flour and set aside.
3. In a large frying pan with a little oil on medium heat, fry the garlic and french shallots for a couple of minutes.
4. Remove and place into the casserole dish.
5. Add a little more oil to the pan, and fry the carrots and celery for a couple of minutes, then add to the casserole dish.
6. Increase the heat of the pan to medium/high. Add half the butter and half the beef. Fry for about 2 minutes until the beef is sealed, then add to the casserole dish.
7. Add the last of the butter and beef and repeat the process; then add beef to the casserole dish.
8. In the pan, add the beef stock, red wine, tomato paste and cracked black pepper. Heat until very hot, then add into the casserole dish.
9. Place the thyme sprigs on top of the casserole. Cover with the lid (or foil if you don't have a lid) and place in the oven for 2 hours. When ready, remove the thyme sprigs and serve.

Crispy Skin Salmon with Pea Purée

Serve the salmon with the pea purée and steamed or boiled baby potatoes.

200 g (7 oz) frozen peas

1 tbsp unsalted butter

2 scallions (spring onions), chopped

125 ml (4 fl oz) low sodium chicken stock

Oil, for frying

4 x 200g (7 oz) salmon fillet with skin on

Boiled baby potatoes, to serve if desired

Serves 4

1. Put the peas in a saucepan of boiling water and boil for 2–3 minutes, until cooked. Drain and reserve in a bowl.
2. Return saucepan to medium-low heat, add butter and chopped scallions, and cook gently for 2 minutes.
3. Add chicken stock and heat for 1 minute.
4. Remove from heat and add the peas back to the saucepan.
5. Using a stick blender, blend all ingredients until smooth. Set aside until the salmon is ready to serve.
6. In a pan heat a little oil to medium-hot heat.
7. Add the salmon, skin side down and cook for 3–4 minutes. Turn the salmon over and cook another 2 minutes.

Portuguese Style Chicken

Note that you can use the whole cilantro bunch in this recipe, the leaves, stems, roots – toss it all in the food processor! Just make sure that it is washed thoroughly before using.
I have used wings and thighs for this recipe, but you could use any cut you prefer.

1 red bell pepper (capsicum)
1 large red chili
3 garlic cloves, peeled
Whole bunch cilantro (coriander)
½ lemon, zest and juice
½ tsp ground cilantro (coriander) seeds
900 g (2 lb) chicken pieces

Serves 4

1. To roast the bell pepper, place on a baking tray in a preheated 200°C (400°F) oven for about 20 minutes, or until the skin starts to blacken. Allow to cool slightly then peel off the skin and chop roughly.
2. To make the marinade, add all the ingredients, other than the chicken, to a food processor, process until combined. (Reserve a little cilantro leaf for garnish).
3. Put the chicken pieces into a bowl, and pour the marinade over. Make sure all the chicken is coated in marinade. Cover with plastic wrap and leave in the fridge for at least 2 hours (overnight is better).
4. Take the chicken out of the fridge 20 minutes before you are ready to cook, so that it can come back to room temperature.
5. Heat a grill pan to medium heat, cook the chicken pieces for about 15 minutes, turning over a few times, and basting about half way through with any marinade left in the bowl.
6. You can check the chicken is cooked thoroughly by cutting into a piece and making sure there is no pink inside.
7. Garnish with a little fresh cilantro.

Spiced Lamb Cutlets with Mint Yogurt

These tender marinated lamb cutlets soak up the flavors of the spices so well, and everyone loves a dipping sauce!

Dipping yogurt

125 g (4.5 oz) natural yogurt

1 tbsp honey

3 tbsp chopped mint

Lamb cutlets

2 garlic cloves, crushed

85 ml (2.9 fl oz) olive oil

12 lamb cutlets

2 tbsp allspice

1 tbsp ground cilantro (coriander) seeds

2 tbsp cumin

2 tbsp sumac

Serves 4

Dipping yogurt method

1. Combine the yogurt with the honey and chopped mint, mix well. Keep chilled in the refrigerator until ready to serve.

Lamb cutlets

2. Mix the crushed garlic and oil in a bowl, then brush onto each side of the cutlets.
3. Combine the allspice, cilantro, cumin and sumac in a shallow bowl.
4. Press each cutlet into the spice mixture, coating well on both sides.
5. Heat a grill pan to medium high. Cook the cutlets for about 4 minutes on each side, for medium-rare.
6. Remove from pan and place on a plate, loosely cover with foil. Allow lamb to rest for 5 minutes before serving with the yogurt.

Butter Chicken

I always used to make butter chicken with sauce from a jar before realizing how much sodium was in them. I also didn't realize that it is quite simple to make your own – don't be scared by the long list of ingredients! You will find that you use spices regularly if you are cooking without salt. If you are making this for children to eat, I'd suggest leaving out the chili powder.

Oil for frying

1 brown onion, chopped

2 garlic cloves, finely chopped

2 tbsp finely grated fresh ginger

2 tsp ground cumin

2 tsp ground cilantro (coriander) seeds

1 tsp garam masala

1 tsp sweet paprika powder

½ tsp turmeric

¼ tsp chili powder

500 g (17.5 oz) skinless chicken thighs, cubed

2 tbsp lemon juice

400 g (14 oz) tin tomato purée

2 tbsp tomato paste

20 g (¾ oz) unsalted butter

1 bay leaf

150 g (5 oz) Greek yogurt

Rice and cilantro (coriander) to serve if desired

Serves 4

1. In a pan on medium heat, add a little oil with the onions. Gently fry them for a couple of minutes to soften them.
2. Add the garlic and ginger, fry for about a minute. Add the cumin, cilantro, garam masala, paprika, turmeric and chili. Fry for another minute. Remove everything from the pan and set aside in a bowl.
3. Increase the pan heat to medium high, and cook the chicken in small batches for a couple of minutes each side until the chicken is sealed and browned on the outside. Place the chicken in the bowl with the onion mix while you cook the other batches.
4. Once the chicken is all sealed and removed from the pan, add the lemon juice and scrape the pan to loosen all the flavors from the cooking so far.
5. The onion mix and chicken can then be returned to the pan. Finally add the tomato purée, tomato paste, butter and bay leaf.
6. Stir to combine and leave at a gentle simmer for 15 minutes, stirring occasionally.
7. When ready to serve, add the yogurt and mix well.
8. Remove from the heat and remove the bay leaf. Serve with rice and fresh cilantro

American Pork Ribs

These are one of my absolute favorites! Beautiful slow cooked ribs that just fall off the bone, in a rich sweet and spicy tomato sauce.
There are a couple of low sodium tomato sauces on the market now, generally found in supermarkets.

1 kg (2¼ lb) pork ribs
300 ml (10 fl oz) tomato sauce
  (low sodium)
125 ml (4 fl oz) malt vinegar
50 g (2 oz) brown sugar
1 tbsp golden syrup
½ tsp Chinese five spice
¼ tsp cayenne pepper

Serves 4

1. Preheat the oven to 180°C (350°F).
2. Place the pork ribs into a large bowl.
3. In a saucepan over low heat, add all the remaining ingredients.
4. On a low heat, stir until the sugar and syrup has dissolved. Set aside about 4 tablespoons of the marinade in a small container for use later.
5. Pour the remaining marinade over the ribs and set aside for about 30 minutes. (A few hours in the fridge is better, if you have the time).
6. Remove the ribs from the bowl and place onto a baking tray. Make sure they are all well coated in the marinade.
7. Cover with foil and bake for 2 hours, turning the ribs over after 1 hour (keep foil on for entire cooking time).
8. When ready, remove the ribs and place on serving platter.
9. Take the remaining 4 tablespoons of marinate and brush over ribs. Serve while hot.

Beef Filled Bell Pepper

My mother in law, Zivka, first taught me her version of this European dish many years ago. Now I have created my own low sodium version. Try and select bell peppers that are all about the same size, and that have a flattish base so they can stand up in the casserole dish.

Bell Peppers

4 red bell peppers (capsicum), medium size

1 garlic clove, crushed

1 celery stick, diced finely

½ a carrot, peeled and diced finely

500 g (17.5 oz) beef mince

1 tbsp malt vinegar

1 tsp smoked paprika powder

Bell Pepper method

1. Preheat the oven to 180°C (350°F).
2. Prepare the bell peppers by cutting off the tops (keep the tops) and scraping out the seeds from the inside. Place the bell peppers inside a deep casserole dish.
3. Finely dice the useable part from the tops of the bell peppers and set aside.
4. In a medium hot frying pan add a little oil, half the garlic, half the celery and half the carrot. Fry for a few minutes until they start to soften and begin to brown slightly. Remove from the pan and set aside in a bowl.
5. Brown the beef in the pan, stirring frequently, for a few minutes. Be sure to break up the mince with your spoon so that it is not in large clumps. Add the malt vinegar and 1 teaspoon of paprika powder, simmer for 2 minutes then add the garlic, celery and carrot back to the pan. Stir well and simmer for a further minute.
6. Remove from the heat, and use the mixture to fill the hollow bell peppers.

continued over the page ...

Sauce

Oil for frying
1 small onion, chopped finely
1 garlic clove, crushed
½ a carrot, diced finely
1 celery stick, diced finely
400 g (14 oz) passata
Freshly ground black pepper
25 g (1 oz) unsalted butter
2 tbsp all-purpose (plain) flour
1 tsp smoked paprika powder
125 ml (4 fl oz) red wine
200 ml (7 fl oz) water

Serves 4

Sauce method

1. To make the sauce, return the same frying pan (no need to clean it) to a medium high heat with a little oil (if needed). Add the onion, garlic, the remaining celery, the remaining carrot and the diced bell pepper lids. Gently fry for 3–4 minutes then add the passata. Grind in some black pepper, stir well, simmer for 1 minute then turn off the heat.

2. In a small saucepan on medium heat, add the butter, flour and paprika powder. Stir and cook for 2–3 minutes, stirring frequently. Using a whisk, slowly add the wine, whisking constantly so that lumps don't form. Then very slowly add the water, whisking constantly, creating a paste.

3. When all the water has been added, pour the paste into the passata mixture. Use the whisk to combine well.

4. Pour the sauce all around the capsicums. Place a lid on the dish (or foil if you don't have one) and bake in the oven for 50 minutes.

Duck with Plum Sauce

Crispy skin duck looks amazing and is superb for entertaining. Try matching it with my butter bean mash – I find this helps cut through the richness of the duck and plum sauce.

4 x duck breast, skin on
½ tsp Chinese five
   spice
8 plums
250 ml (8 fl oz) red wine
I tsp unsalted butter

Butter Bean Mash, to
   serve (page 162)

Serves 4

1. Dry the duck breasts with paper towel and then place the breasts skin side down on a few layers of clean paper towel. Place into the refrigerator for a minimum of 2 hours, during this time, change the paper towels a couple of times. This will help to achieve a beautiful crispy skin.
2. About 30 minutes prior to cooking, remove duck from the refrigerator and rub all over with the Chinese five spice. Cover and leave at room temperature.
3. Halve the plums, remove the pips. Slice 2 plums into thin segments, set aside.
4. Dice the 6 remaining plums and place into a small frying pan with the red wine. Bring to a gentle simmer, then cover with a lid and leave for 20 minutes.
5. Use a non-stick heavy based frying pan, and bring to a medium hot heat. Place the duck breasts skin side down for about 6 minutes. The fat should have rendered and the skin should be golden and crisp.
6. Reduce the heat a little, turn the breasts over and cook for a further 5 minutes.
7. The duck should be medium firm to touch when cooked. Remove from heat, place on a warm plate, cover loosely with aluminium foil. Rest for 3–4 minutes.
8. While the duck is resting pour off the excess fat and oil from the pan, and then add the red wine and cooked plums. Stir to combine with the pan juices.
9. Add the plum segments and simmer for 3 minutes, then remove the segments and place onto a warm plate.
10. Pour any juices that have come from the duck breast into the sauce and stir in the butter.
11. Remove this mix from the pan, and purée with a blender. Strain the purée through a fine sieve and the sauce is ready.
12. Serve the duck breast together with the plum segments and sauce.

Easy Chicken Curry

This recipe is for mild curry, add more chili if you prefer hotter. Ajowan seeds can be found in delicatessens or Indian food stores. Some supermarkets may stock them also.

500 g (17.5 oz) skinless chicken thighs, cubed
2 tbsp all-purpose (plain) flour
Olive oil, for frying
1 large brown onion, chopped
1 tbsp finely grated ginger
3 garlic cloves, crushed
400 g (14 oz) can of chopped tomatoes
2 tsp cumin seeds, ground
1 tsp ajowan seeds, ground
½ tsp ground chili powder
½ tsp cracked black pepper
1 tsp ground cardamon
½ tsp cinnamon
½ tsp nutmeg
1 tsp ground turmeric
180 ml (6 fl oz) water

Rice, to serve if desired.
Flat bread, to serve (page 27)

Serves 4

1. Place the flour into a bowl, and toss the chicken pieces until all are lightly coated.
2. Heat a frying pan to high and add a little olive oil.
3. Cook the chicken in small batches, to seal and just brown the pieces a little. Set aside in a bowl.
4. Reduce the pan heat to medium adding a little oil if needed. Fry the onion for a 2–3 minutes, to soften, stirring occasionally. Add the ginger and garlic, fry for a further 2 minutes then remove from the heat.
5. In a food processor, place the onion mix, the chopped tomatoes, cumin, ajowan, chili, pepper, cardamon, cinnamon, nutmeg, turmeric. Blend to a paste. Add the water and blend again.
6. Return the chicken to the frying pan along with the mix from the food processor.
7. Stir well and bring to a gentle simmer.
8. Leave for 45 minutes, uncovered, stirring occasionally.
9. Serve with rice, and flat bread (page 27).

Roasted Whole Chicken with Sage Butter

You can check the chicken is ready by piercing the thigh with a skewer – if the juices run out clear, it is ready. If there is any pink or blood, it needs more roasting.

Getting the herb butter under the skin does take a little time as you need to be careful not to rip the chicken skin, but please persevere because it really helps to keep the chicken moist and delivers wonderful flavor. The chicken carcass from this roast is great to keep and make some low sodium chicken stock (page 195)

1 whole chicken, (approximately 1.8 kg, 4 lb) rinsed and dried

1 bunch rosemary

2 bunch sage leaves

2 garlic clove, sliced

75 g (2.5 oz) unsalted butter, at room temperature

2 tsp olive oil

Serves 4–6

1. Preheat the oven to 180°C (350°F).
2. Take half the rosemary stalks and half the sage leaves, and place whole inside the chicken cavity. Place the sliced garlic inside the cavity also.
3. Roughly chop the remaining sage leaves, and strip remaining rosemary from the stalk. In a bowl, mix together with the unsalted butter.
4. Gently separate the chicken skin from the two breast fillets by easing your fingers between the meat and skin. Start at the cavity end, and carefully lift the skin away from the meat to create space for the butter. Be very careful not to rip the skin.
5. Push the butter mixture under the skin, making sure it is evenly distributed. Secure the skin at the cavity end with a couple of toothpicks. Drizzle a little olive oil over the skin of the chicken so it is all coated.
6. Use a baking dish with a rack. Place the chicken on the rack, put the baking dish in the oven and roast for 1.5 hours.

T-bone Steak with Mushroom Sauce

Nothing beats a creamy mash to soak up yummy sauces like this – you should definitely try my Parsnip Purée (page 152) with these T-bones, or even my Butter Bean Mash (page 162) for something different.

4 x 300 g (10.5 oz) beef t-bone
   steaks

Mushroom sauce
4 cloves garlic, crushed
200 g (7 oz) swiss brown
   mushrooms
60 g (2 oz) unsalted butter
250 ml (8fl oz) thickened cream
Olive oil, for frying
Cracked black pepper

Steamed green beans to serve, if
   desired
Parsnip purée to serve, if desired
   (see page 152)

Serves 4

1. Prepare a large frying pan to high heat with a little oil.
2. Add the steaks and cook for about 2–3 minutes on each side, or until cooked to your liking.
3. Set aside on a warm plate covered loosely in tin foil to rest, while you make the sauce.
4. In the same pan (do not clean) reduce the heat to medium add the garlic and mushrooms, fry for a minute.
5. Add the butter, and fry for 3–4 minutes until the mushrooms have softened.
6. Add the cream and stir through, making sure to scrape the bottom of the pan to remove flavor. Remove from the heat. The cream will turn a beautiful brown once mixed with the pan juices and mushrooms.
7. Add cracked black pepper to taste, serve immediately with the steak and sides of your choice.

Chicken Thyme Casserole

Chicken wings, drumstick or thigh all work well for this recipe.

700 g (1.5 lb) chicken pieces
2 french onions, chopped
    roughly
3 garlic cloves, chopped
125 ml (4 fl oz) dry white wine
375 ml (12 fl oz) low sodium
    chicken stock
The zest and juice of a lemon
1 large potato, chopped into
    2 cm (¾ in) cubes
2 tbsp fresh thyme, chopped
Oil for frying
Freshly ground black pepper

Serves 4

1. Preheat oven to 180°C (350°F).
2. On the stove top, heat a little oil in a flameproof casserole dish to medium high heat.
3. In small batches, brown the chicken for around 2 minutes each side, until browned. Once all the chicken is browned, set aside in another bowl.
4. Decrease heat to medium-low, add the onion and garlic and fry gently for 1 minute, taking care to not let the onion brown.
5. Return the chicken to the casserole dish, add the white wine, stock, lemon zest, lemon juice, potato, thyme and black pepper.
6. Increase the heat to high and bring to the boil.
7. Remove from the stove top, cover with lid or foil, and bake in oven for 40 minutes.

Barramundi Fillets with Walnut and Cream Sauce

I really wanted to create something different to go with these fillets. The walnuts give that beautiful nutty flavor, as well as some texture to the smooth cream.
You could use other types of white fish if you prefer, just keep the fillets under 1.5 cm (⅝ in) thickness.

4 x barramundi fillets, no thicker than 2 cm (1 in)
2 tsp plus 1 tsp olive oil
2 cloves garlic, finely chopped
50 g (2 oz) walnuts
125 ml (4 fl oz) white wine
2 tsp lemon juice
Cracked black pepper
125 ml (4 fl oz) thickened cream

Serves 4

1. Preheat the grill to very hot.
2. Lay the fish fillets on a flat tray lined with baking paper, then brush them with 2 teaspoons of oil. Place them under the grill about 10 cm (4 in) from heat. Cook for 5–6 minutes, not turning them over, until the fish is ready and flakes easily.
3. While the fish is cooking, prepare a frying pan to medium high heat, with the remaining teaspoon of oil. Add the garlic and cook for 1 minute, then add the walnuts. Stir and fry for a couple of minutes to toast the nuts.
4. Add the white wine, lemon juice, pepper and then the cream. Stir to combine and remove from the heat.
5. Serve poured over the fish fillets.

White Wine Lamb Shanks

This tender, juicy lamb is best served with Parsnip Purée (page 152) and Green Beans (page 156).

4 Lamb shanks

2 tbsp all-purpose (plain) flour

1 tsp plus ½ tsp cracked black pepper

2 tbsp plus 1 tbsp vegetable oil

4 x lamb shank, approximately 1.7 kg (3.8 lbs)

125 ml (4 fl oz) plus 125 ml (4 fl oz) plus 125ml (4 fl oz) white wine

4 medium carrots, peeled and chopped into large pieces

8 shallots, peeled

3 garlic cloves, crushed

1 tsp fennel seeds, lightly ground

1 litre (1¾ pints) low sodium vegetable stock

4 tbsp tomato paste

8 sage leaves, roughly chopped

Parsnip Purée and Green Beans to serve, if desired

Serves 4

1. Preheat the oven to 180°C (350°F).
2. In a bowl mix the flour and ½ teaspoon cracked black pepper and then use this to lightly dust the surface of the lamb shanks.
3. Prepare a frying pan with 2 tablespoons of the oil, to high heat.
4. Add 2 of the shanks, and fry, turning frequently until the surface has caramelized and is a nice golden brown.
5. Remove from pan and place in an oven safe casserole dish. Repeat for the other 2 shanks. Deglaze the pan by pouring in 125 ml (4 fl oz) of the white wine, and scraping the bottom of the pan to loosen all the flavor. Pour over the shanks.
6. Add the remaining tablespoon of oil to the pan, heat to medium high and add the carrots and shallots.
7. Fry for about 5 minutes, turning frequently until they begin to caramelize.
8. Turn the heat down to medium and add the garlic cloves. Fry for another 2 minutes, and then add the ground fennel seeds, frying for a further minute.
9. Add this mix into the casserole dish. Deglaze the pan again with another 125 ml (4 fl oz) of white wine, add this to the casserole dish also.
10. In a jug, add the remaining 125 ml (4 fl oz) white wine, the remaining teaspoon of cracked black pepper, vegetable stock, tomato paste and sage leaves. Stir well, then pour over the shanks and vegetables.
11. The shanks and vegetables should be largely covered by the wine and stock mix, if not, perhaps try a smaller, deeper casserole dish. Put a lid on the casserole dish and bake for 2 hours, turning the shanks over after an hour.

SIDES

Minted Peas

You can easily substitute or add other peas like sugar snap, or fresh instead of frozen, to make this quick and easy side dish.

130 g (4.5 oz) frozen green peas
130 g (4.5 oz) fresh snow peas
1 tbsp unsalted butter
2 tbsp chopped mint

Serves 4

1. Place the frozen green peas in a saucepan of boiling water and cook for 3 minutes, adding the fresh snow peas for the last minute of cooking.
2. Drain and refresh in a large bowl of chilled water. Drain and transfer to a serving bowl.
3. Melt the butter in a small saucepan over medium heat. Remove from the heat, add the mint and stir.
4. Pour the butter mix into the pea bowl and stir to coat all the peas in the butter.

Potato and Rosemary Bake

If you cannot find any low sodium cheese, you can easily leave it out altogether, but still bake for the final 20 minutes uncovered.

If you have a food processor, you can use the slicing attachment for the potatoes instead of slicing by hand – this saves a lot of time!

1 kg (2.2 lb) white potatoes

1 small brown onion, finely chopped

1 garlic clove, crushed

1 sprig rosemary, leaves stripped and chopped

Cracked black pepper

300 ml (10 fl oz) thickened cream

150 ml (5 fl oz) milk

30 g (1 oz) low sodium cheese, grated

Serves 6

1. Preheat the oven to 200°C (400°F).
2. Peel the potatoes, and slice (approximately 5 mm (¼ in) thickness). Place into an ovenproof dish.
3. In a small jug place the onion, garlic, rosemary and black pepper; then pour in the cream and milk. Mix well, and then pour over the potatoes.
4. Stir the potatoes so that they are all coated in the mixture, then cover and bake for 35 minutes.
5. Remove from the oven and stir again so that all the potatoes are thoroughly coated in the cream. Sprinkle the grated cheese on top, then bake uncovered for 20 minutes.

Tabouli

To avoid the tomatoes getting soggy, don't add the dressing until just before you are ready to serve. Bulgur can be found in the supermarket near the pasta and rice, or sometimes in the health food section. You could also use couscous as an alternative.

50 g (2 oz) uncooked bulgur
2 bunches of parsley (about
  180 g/6 oz)
3 tomatoes (about 270 g/9.5 oz),
  finely chopped
2 tbsp chopped mint
¼ red onion (50 g/2 oz), finely
  chopped
2 tbsp olive oil
1 tbsp lemon juice
1 garlic clove, crushed

Serves 4

1. Prepare the bulgur by placing it in a small bowl with 125 ml (4 fl oz) of freshly boiled water. Set aside for a few minutes to soak up the water.
2. Meanwhile in a large bowl place the parsley, tomatoes, mint and onion. Mix gently.
3. In a little jug, mix the oil, lemon juice and crushed garlic.
4. Once the bulgur has soaked up all the water, add it to the parsley bowl. Then pour in the oil mix and stir everything to combine.

Parsnip Purée with Crispy Parsnip Chips

These parsnip chips are a nice way of adding a little crunch into the smooth parsnip purée! Plus, they also look great sprinkled on top.

1 kg (2¼ lb) parsnip
125 ml (4 fl oz) thickened cream
Oil for frying

Serves 4

1. Peel the parsnips, then cut in half. Set aside one half parsnip.
2. With the remaining halves, remove the core part, then chop into chunks. Place into a saucepan full of boiling water, boil for 15 minutes. Drain, and process into a smooth purée.
3. Add the cream and stir to combine.
4. While the parsnip is boiling, you can make the parsnip chips. Take the half parsnip you set aside earlier.
5. Slice very finely into strips, or alternatively, use a vegetable peeler to make strips. Take care not to use the core.
6. Use a small frying pan, add vegetable oil to about 1 cm (½ in) depth. Heat to medium high, or if you have a cooking thermometer, the oil should ideally be at 180°C (350°F).
7. Add a few chips at a time and fry until they start to turn golden. This should take less than a minute so watch them carefully!
8. Dry on absorbent paper towel and set aside to use as a garnish on the parsnip purée.

Poppy Seed Pumpkin and Carrot

This quick and easy recipe is a great way to liven up roast pumpkin and carrot with flavor and texture. Use any kind of pumpkin you prefer.

500 g (17.5 oz) pumpkin
500 g (17.5 oz) carrot
2 tbsp olive oil
2 tbsp poppy seeds

Serves 4

1. Preheat oven to 200°C (400°F).
2. Peel the pumpkin and carrot, cut roughly into 3 cm (1¼ in) pieces, then place in a large saucepan of boiling water.
3. Simmer for approximately 5 minutes.
4. Drain the vegetables, and place pieces onto a baking tray, in a single layer.
4. Drizzle olive oil, then poppy seeds, over vegetable pieces. Toss to coat evenly.
5. Bake for 15 minutes or until cooked through.

Green Beans with Cranberries and Lemon Thyme

The slight sweetness of the cranberries really suits the tangy lemon thyme - something different to the plain green beans that usually appear on the table!

200 g (7 oz) fresh green beans

1 tsp olive oil

25 g (1 oz) unsalted butter

25 g (1 oz) dried cranberries, chopped roughly

1 large sprig lemon thyme, chopped finely

1. Clean and trim the ends of the beans.
2. Heat a grill pan to medium high and add the oil.
3. Cook the beans for about 2 minutes, then add the butter, cranberries and lemon thyme.
4. Cook for a further minute once the butter has melted, tossing the beans through the butter to combine.
5. Serve while hot.

Serves 4

Zucchini with Paprika and Ground Cumin

Make sure you use a ridged grill pan to achieve these lovely criss cross patterns.

1 kg (2¼ lb) zucchini (courgette)
(about 6)
1 tsp cumin seeds
2 tbsp olive oil
½ tsp paprika

Lemon wedges, to serve

Serves 4–6

1. Cut the zucchini into slices lengthwise, about 5 mm (¼ in) thickness.
2. Grind the cumin seeds with a mortar and pestle, then in a little jug, mix together with the oil and paprika. Pour the oil mix onto a flat plate and spread into a thin layer.
3. Press one side only of each slice of zucchini onto the oil and spice mix.
4. Heat a grill pan to medium high, cook for a couple of minutes, oil side down until grill marks appear. Then same side down, rotate by 90°. This will give you the golden criss cross pattern.
5. Flip the slices and cook for a further one minute. Serve with the patterned side up while still warm.

Asparagus with Lemon Tarragon Butter

These vibrant asparagus have a delicious zesty flavor, look amazing and are ready in literally just minutes.

2 bunch of asparagus (about 20 stalks)

1 tsp olive oil

1 tbsp lemon juice

20 g (¾ oz) unsalted butter

1 tbsp chopped fresh tarragon

Serves 4

1. Trim the asparagus to remove the dry part at the end of the stalk.
2. Heat a grill pan to medium high heat with the oil. Cook the asparagus for 2 minutes, shaking them frequently in the pan to ensure even cooking.
3. Add the lemon juice, butter and tarragon. Once the butter has melted, remove from the heat.
4. Ensure all the asparagus is coated in the butter, and serve hot.

Butter Bean Mash

This side dish makes for an interesting change from the standard potato mash — and is also much faster
if you are short on time!
You can add more or less water depending on your preference for thick or thin mash.
Make sure the butter beans are a no added salt variety.

2 x 400 g (14 oz) tin of butter
   beans, drained and rinsed well
1 tsp garlic powder
2 tsp olive oil
Juice of half a lemon
2 tbsp water

Serves 4

1. Place all of the ingredients into a food processor and process until
   combined to a smooth consistency.
2. Transfer the mash to a saucepan, gently heat over low heat and
   serve once warmed through.

Coconut Rice

Coconut rice is a nice change from plain boiled rice, and is well suited to dishes with asian flavors. Try it with my Chicken Skewers with Satay Sauce (page 30) .
Make sure that you rinse the rice before cooking, this removes some of the starch and means there is less chance of it being clumpy when cooked.

600 g (21 oz) jasmine rice
2 x 400 ml (13.5 fl oz) can
   coconut milk
500 ml (16 fl oz) water

Serves 6

1. Rinse the jasmine rice in a fine sieve or colander, under cold water. Set aside.
2. In a large saucepan, bring the coconut milk and water to the boil, stirring occasionally, then add the rice.
3. Return to the boil, then reduce to low heat. Cover and simmer gently for 18–20 minutes, or until the rice is fluffy and tender.
4. Remove from the heat and let stand for 5 minutes with the lid on. Fluff the rice with a fork and serve.

Dutch Carrots with Roasted Sesame and Honey

Add a little sweetness, texture and color to your plate with this tasty side!

2 x bunches dutch carrots (about 325 g/11.5 oz) per bunch

1 tbsp sesame seeds

25 g (1 oz) unsalted butter

1 tsp honey

Serves 4

1. Wash and trim the greenery from the carrots, then set aside.
2. In a dry, deep frying pan on medium heat, lightly roast the sesame seeds for a couple of minutes, shaking frequently.
3. Add the butter, allow to melt, then reduce the heat to low. Then add the honey and stir well. Add the carrots and stir well to coat them. Cook for 5–7 minutes, or until the carrots are soft.
3. Remove and serve while still warm.

Lemon Pepper Button Mushrooms

Try to turn over the mushrooms just once, this way you will achieve the lovely grill markings over their tops.

200 g (7 oz) white button mushrooms
25 g (1 oz) unsalted butter, melted
½ tsp cracked black pepper
Juice of half a lemon

Serves 4

1. Clean the mushrooms and trim the stalk to be level with the base of the mushroom.
2. In a mixing bowl, add the melted butter, black pepper and lemon juice. Stir well. Add the mushrooms and toss them around in the mixture, ensuring they are well coated.
3. Heat a grill pan to medium. Add half the mushroom mixture and fry for 2 minutes. Turn the mushrooms over and fry the other side for a further 2 minutes.
4. Remove mushrooms and set aside, repeat with remaining mushroom mix.
5. Serve while hot.

SWEETS

Pancakes with Lemon Curd

It is so nice to make your own curd, no additives, no preservatives – it will also keep well for up to a week in the refrigerator if you transfer it to a sterilized jar.

It is definitely a bit tedious standing over the stove top and whisking continuously while you wait for the curd to thicken – but it is worth it – otherwise the curd will become lumpy!

Pancakes

110 g (4 oz) all-purpose (plain) flour
1 egg
250 ml (8 fl oz) milk
Unsalted butter, for frying

Makes about 4 pancakes, in a pan of 20 cm (8 in) diameter

Lemon curd

100 g (3.5 oz) unsalted butter
125 ml (4 fl oz) lemon juice
4 egg yolks
100 g (3.5 oz) superfine (caster) sugar

Makes about 250 ml (8 fl oz).

To make pancakes

1. Sift the flour into a mixing bowl.
2. Make a well in the centre, add the egg and whisk until combined.
3. Slowly add the milk, whisking continuously to avoid lumps. Let the mixture stand for 5–10 minutes.
4. Heat a heavy based frying pan and add a teaspoon of unsalted butter.
5. Pour in enough mixture to cover most of the base of the pan. Cook until small bubbles form and begin to pop, then turn over the pancake to cook for 10–20 seconds on the other side.

To make lemon curd

1. Prepare a large bowl full of ice in the sink. Prepare a small saucepan about ¼ full of simmering water.
2. In a small pan (or a bowl in the microwave) melt the butter, then add the lemon juice. Stir to combine and set aside.
3. In a heatproof bowl, add the yolks and sugar and whisk them to combine. Then slowly pour in the butter and lemon mixture, whisking continuously to combine. Set up the heatproof bowl to sit on top of your saucepan of simmering water, making sure that the water does not touch the bottom of the bowl.
4. Using the whisk, stir the mixture continuously for about 7–9 minutes until the mixture thickens. Once thick, remove from the heat and place the bowl with curd on top of your ice bowl, so that the mixture can chill quickly. Serve the pancakes and curd with some fresh blueberries, if desired.

Orange Chocolate Mousse

This mousse is very rich – just the way I like it. It does need a couple of hours in the fridge to set, or better still, prepare this the night before and keep covered in the fridge until serving.
For best results, beat the egg whites in a stainless steel bowl.
After grating the orange rind, I then chop it on a board so that it becomes super fine.

200 g (7 oz) good quality cooking chocolate (70% cocoa)

4 eggs, separated, at room temperature

75 g (3 oz) superfine (caster) sugar

2 tsp orange rind, very finely grated

60 ml (2 fl oz) orange juice, strained

300 ml (10 fl oz) thickened cream

Serves 4–6 depending on size

1. Break up the chocolate and place into a heatproof bowl, sitting over a saucepan of gently simmering water. Make sure that the bowl does not touch the water. Stir until melted and set aside to cool slightly.
2. In a bowl, mix together the egg yolks, a third of the sugar, the orange rind and orange juice, until well combined.
3. In a separate bowl, beat the cream until just thick.
4. In a separate clean, dry bowl, beat the egg whites and remaining sugar until stiff peaks form.
5. Add the melted chocolate to the egg yolk mixture and whisk until combined.
6. Whisk the thickened cream to the chocolate mixture.
7. With a metal spoon, gently fold in the egg whites to the chocolate mixture, taking care not to overwork the mixture.
8. Pour the mousse into 6 dishes or glasses. Cover with plastic wrap and chill in the refrigerator for at least 2 hours.

Rice Pudding

Rice pudding is a real comfort food for a cold winter night. It reminds me of my Mum, who used to make it for me and my sisters as kids.

300 g (10.5 oz) white long grain rice, uncooked

1 litre (1¾ pints) milk

300 ml (10 fl oz) thickened cream

1 tsp vanilla essence

70 g (2.5 oz) white sugar

¼ tsp cinnamon

1 tbsp unsalted butter

Serves 6

1. Preheat the oven to 180°C (350°F).
2. Add all the ingredients except the cinnamon and butter to a saucepan.
3. Bring to a simmer, then pour into an ovenproof dish.
4. Place the unsalted butter on top of the pudding, in the middle, then put on the lid.
5. Bake in the oven for 55 minutes.
6. Sprinkle the cinnamon over the pudding and serve warm.

Baked Apples

You will need an apple corer for this recipe. You can use maple syrup in place of golden syrup, and swap the currants for sultanas, if you prefer.
This recipe is my variation of our 'Grandpa Mike's' original, from his childhood.

4 green apples
2 tbsp plus 1 tbsp currants
2 tsp white sugar
1 tsp cinnamon
4 tsp plus 1 tbsp golden syrup
6 strawberries, hulled and sliced
Ice cream, to serve

Serves 4

1. Preheat the oven to 180°C (350°F).
2. Wash the apples and remove the cores. Using a sharp knife, prick the surface of each apple a few times all over. This will help to stop the skin bursting while baking.
3. Place the apples into a small baking tray.
4. In a little bowl mix together the currants, sugar and cinnamon. Then, using a teaspoon, stuff into the apple holes, dividing the mixture equally between the apples.
5. Drizzle a teaspoon of golden syrup into the top of each apple cavity. Take the remaining tablespoon of golden syrup and drizzle it into the bottom of the baking tray.
6. Scatter the strawberry slices around the apples. Scatter the remaining tablespoon of currants into the tray also.
7. Pour a little water into the tray, about 1 cm (½ in) depth.
8. Bake for about 35 minutes, or until the apples are soft and a little wrinkled, but not falling apart.
9. Serve the apples with some of the strawberry mixture from the tray, and some ice cream.

White Wine Poached Pears

The cinnamon stick can be reserved for garnish if you desire.
If you prefer the poaching liquid a little thicker and sweeter, more like syrup, you can reduce it down by simmering for a few extra minutes with the lid off, once the pears have been removed.

500 ml (17 fl oz) water

250 ml (8.5 fl oz) dry white wine

55 g (2 oz) superfine (caster) sugar

½ vanilla bean, split lengthways and scraped

2 cloves

1 cinnamon stick

4 pears, peeled (cored if you prefer, but this is not essential)

Serves 4

1. Place all of the ingredients except the pears, into a saucepan. Simmer until the sugar is dissolved, stirring occasionally.
2. Add the pears and simmer for 30 minutes, with the lid on. Turn the pears around 2 or 3 times while cooking.
3. Once the pears are soft (it may take a little more or less times depending on the ripeness of your pears), remove the cinnamon stick, cloves and vanilla bean.
3. Place the pears into 4 bowls, and spoon in some of the poaching liquid to serve.

Flourless Chocolate Pecan Cake

This is a beautifully dense, gluten free cake. Serve with plain whipped cream or good double cream to cut through the richness.

Try to buy good quality cooking chocolate, it really makes a huge difference to the taste.

200 g (7 oz) dark cooking chocolate

150 g (5 oz) unsalted butter

110 g (4 oz) superfine (caster) sugar

4 eggs, separated, at room temperature

1 tsp vanilla essence

65 g (2.3 oz) pecans, chopped roughly

150 g (5 oz) hazelnut meal (ground hazelnuts)

1 tbsp cocoa powder

Whipped cream to serve, if desired.

Serves 8

1. Preheat oven to 180°C (350°F).
2. Prepare 20 cm (8 in) round cake tin by greasing and lining with baking paper.
3. Break the chocolate into pieces and place in a heatproof bowl over a saucepan of simmering water. Stir until chocolate is melted and then set aside to cool a little.
4. Cream the butter and sugar until pale.
5. Add the egg yolks, vanilla essence, pecans, hazelnut meal and cocoa powder, stir to combine.
6. Pour the melted chocolate into the mixture and stir to combine.
7. In a new clean bowl, beat the egg whites until stiff peaks form.
8. Gently fold the egg whites into the chocolate mixture, until just combined. Try not to overwork the mixture at this point.
9. Pour mixture into the prepared tin, and bake for 50 minutes.

Warm Lemon Sago Pudding

Sago can be found in most supermarkets. It has an interesting feel and texture – a nice change from the standard desserts you are probably used to making.

85 g (3 oz) sago
400 ml (13.5 fl oz) coconut milk
Juice and rind of 1 lemon
1 egg
2 tbsp honey

Serves 4

1. Place the sago in a medium saucepan full of water and bring to a rapid simmer. Continue to simmer for about 25 minutes stirring very frequently to prevent the sago from sticking to the bottom of the pan. When ready, the sago should have turned from white to be translucent.
2. Drain into a fine sieve or colander and rinse under cold water. Transfer sago to a clean bowl.
3. In the same saucepan bring the coconut milk, lemon juice and rind to the boil then remove from the heat immediately.
4. In a large mixing bowl lightly beat the egg. Slowly begin to add small amounts of the milk mixture to the egg, while whisking continuously. Continue adding the milk and whisking until all the milk mixture has been added.
5. Return the milk mixture to the saucepan and add the honey. Stir and simmer gently for 15 minutes until the mixture begins to thicken. It is very important to stir very frequently at this point to avoid lumps forming.
6. Once the mixture thickens, pour it into the sago and mix to combine. Serve immediately.

Mango Sorbet

Sorbet has to be one of the easiest, quickest desserts you can make.
You can easily substitute other frozen fruits to make this sorbet, try cherry (pictured) using the same quantities.

300 g (10.5 oz) frozen mango
  pieces
30 g (1 oz) superfine (caster)
  sugar
1 egg white

Serves 4

1. Add the mango and sugar into a food processor and process until smooth.
2. Add the egg white and process again for about a minute or until the sorbet has become creamy.
3. Enjoy straight away or put into the freezer for a while to make firmer sorbet.

Strawberries in Grand Marnier Syrup

Grand Marnier is an orange flavored cognac liqueur, which is easy to find in most supermarkets or liquor stores.
A super easy adult dessert literally ready in just minutes!

60 ml (2 fl oz) Grand Marnier

2 tsp superfine (caster) sugar

2 tsp water

2 punnet fresh strawberries, sliced

Vanilla ice cream to serve, if desired

Serves 4

1. In a small pan over low heat, add all ingredients except the strawberries.
2. Stir until all the sugar has dissolved, then add the strawberries.
3. Simmer gently for 5 minutes, allowing the strawberries to soak in the syrup and become soft.
4. Serve while still warm with some vanilla ice cream.

Vanilla Panna Cotta with Muesli Toffee

A classic dessert that everyone seems to love.
You can substitute the vanilla bean for 1 teaspoon of vanilla essence. If you prefer a less sweet dessert, simply leave out the toffee, and sprinkle some toasted muesli around the plate for the crunch.

Panna cotta

3 tbsp water

3 tsp gelatin powder

300 ml (10 fl oz) milk

300 ml (10 fl oz) thickened cream

40 g (1.5 oz) superfine (caster) sugar

1 vanilla bean (split and seeds scraped)

Toffee

100 g (3.5 oz) white sugar

2 tbsp water

50 g (2 oz) toasted muesli

Serves 4

Panna cotta method

1. Measure the water into a small bowl, then sprinkle the gelatine over the water. Leave for 5 minutes or until all the gelatin has soaked in.
2. In a heavy based saucepan, on medium heat, add the milk, cream, sugar and vanilla bean seeds. Heat until hot and the sugar has dissolved.
3. Pour the mixture into a jug and allow to cool slightly.
4. Whisk in the gelatin mixture, continue to whisk for about 20 seconds.
5. Pass the mixture through a fine sieve to collect any lumps from the gelatin, and then pour into 4 small ramekins or moulds. Refrigerate until set – at least a few hours – but better overnight.

Toffee method

1. In a pan over medium heat, add the sugar and water. Keep on medium heat, without stirring, until the sugar has dissolved.
2. Then, increase the heat so the mixture gently bubbles. It is very important not to stir the mixture at all. Continue until the mixture turns golden – this will happen quite quickly so you will need to be watching it to make sure it doesn't burn. This process will take about 10–15 minutes.
3. Meanwhile, spread the muesli onto a baking tray.
4. When the toffee is ready, pour it evenly over the muesli and allow to cool and set hard. Break the toffee into shards and use to decorate your panna cotta.

THE BASICS

Low Sodium Vegetable Stock

As well as containers, I also freeze an ice cube tray of stock – having smaller portions available can be handy as well.

2 tbsp olive oil

3 carrots, chopped

3 celery sticks including leaves, chopped

2 brown onions including skins, chopped

6 peppercorns

100 g (3.5 oz) button mushrooms

1 leek, chopped

A small bunch fresh Parsley, chopped

2 bay leaves

2 litres (3½ pints) water

Makes about 1.5 litres
(2½ pints)

1. In a large heavy based pan over medium heat, add the olive oil, then add the carrots, celery, onion and peppercorns.
2. Cook, stirring constantly until very soft. This will take about 10 minutes. Be very careful not to let the vegetables burn.
3. Then add the mushrooms, leek and parsley, cook for a further 2 minutes.
4. Add the bay leaves and water, cover with a lid, and gently simmer for 40 minutes.
5. Remove from the stovetop and separate the stock from the remaining ingredients by pouring through a muslin cloth.
6. This stock can now be used or frozen in containers for later use.

Low Sodium Beef Stock

Ask your butcher to cut the bones into small pieces for you.
If you would like more concentrated stock, continue to simmer for an hour longer to develop the flavor even further.

1.5 kg (3.3 lb) beef bones (marrow bones if possible)
2 large carrots, chopped
1 celery stick leaves included, chopped
2 large onions, chopped
Small bunch of parsley
6 peppercorns
1 garlic clove, bashed in skin
1 sprig of rosemary
1 sprig of thyme
2 fresh bay leaves

Makes about 1.5 litres
(2½ pints)

1. Preheat your oven to 200°C (350°F).
2. Place the beef bones on a roasting tray and bake for 40 minutes.
3. Remove and place the bones in a large saucepan.
4. Pour a little water into the tray and scrape to remove all the flavor from the tray. Pour this into the saucepan.
5. Add the remaining ingredients, and fill with enough cold water to cover everything completely.
6. Bring to a boil, then reduce to a very gentle simmer for 4–5 hours with the lid on, but slightly ajar.
7. Remove the bones, and strain the stock through a muslin cloth.
8. Allow the stock to cool completely, then refrigerate, or freeze for later use. If any fat appears on the surface, skim off.

Low Sodium Chicken Stock

Use the leftover chicken carcass from page 135 to make this flavorsome chicken stock.

1 chicken carcass (use leftovers from page 135)
2 large carrots, chopped
1 celery stick leaves included, chopped
2 large onions, chopped
Small bunch of parsley
6 peppercorns
1 garlic clove, bashed in skin
1 sprig of rosemary
1 sprig of thyme
1 bay leaf

Makes about 1.5 litres (2½ pints)

1. Place the chicken carcass in a large saucepan and fill with enough cold water to cover it completely.
2. Add all the remaining ingredients and bring to the boil.
3. Reduce to a very gentle simmer, for 4 hours with the lid on, but slightly ajar. Occasionally skim the surface of any scum that appears.
4. Remove the carcass and strain the stock through some muslin cloth.
5. If you would like a more concentrated stock, continue to simmer for an hour longer.
6. Allow the stock to cool completely, then refrigerate, or freeze for later use.

Semi-Dried Tomatoes

Use these delicious tomatoes for my Roasted Tomato Soup recipe on page 67,
or Creamy Chicken Pasta on page 99.

1 kg (2.2 oz) roma tomatoes
1 tbsp olive oil
1 tsp garlic powder (or 1 tbsp
   fresh garlic, chopped)
1 tsp dried oregano leaves

Makes approx 400 g (14 oz)

1. Preheat the oven to 150°C (300°F).
2. Line a flat baking tray with baking paper, and then place a rack on
   the tray.
3. Slice the tomatoes in half lengthways, then arrange cut side up on
   the rack.
4. Mix in a small bowl the oil, garlic powder and oregano.
5. Use a pastry brush to smear a little of the olive oil mixture over
   each of the tomatoes, using all the mixture.
6. Bake the tomatoes for 3 hours.
7. The tomatoes can be stored in an airtight container in the fridge
   for up to 3 days.

Low Sodium White Bread

Always remember to buy the best quality flour that you can – this will really have an effect on the quality of your loaf.
It is handy to have the low sodium bread not only to eat as it is, but also to make breadcrumbs.
Just slice off the required amount and put through the food processor until fine.

260 ml (9 fl oz) warm water

1 tbsp milk powder

1 tsp white sugar

2 tbsp unsalted butter, at room temperature

390 g (13.5 oz) bread flour

1¼ tsp dry yeast

Makes 1 medium sized loaf

1. To make this low sodium bread I use a bread maker. Add the water first, then all the remaining ingredients, placing the yeast in last. Select the basic bread cycle and medium color crust.
2. The whole process should take about 3 hours.

ACKNOWLEDGEMENTS

Thank you to:

Dr Philip Cremer, for his initial encouragement and support to even attempt writing this book.

Clare, who has been with me on this journey from the absolute beginning to the end; she is a wonderful photographer and great friend – I couldn't have done this without her.

Mum and Mike, who helped in so many ways to get me over the finish line!

Diane Ward, who listened to my dream and decided to turn it into reality.

To all my family and friends who have encouraged and supported me – thank you.

Finally, there is no possible way I could have written this book without the unconditional support of my husband, Vel. Thank you for believing in me.

Recipe Index